London Dry Gin does not have to be made in London and today Beefeater Gin is the only major premium gin distilled in the heart of the Capital.

THE QUINTESSENTIAL LONDON DRY GIN

Heritage, quality and London provenance has made Beefeater one of the world's most revered gins.

London Dry Gin is officially defined as a type of distilled gin that is made by redistilling spirit and natural flavourings, principally juniper berries. London Dry Gin does not have to be made in London and today Beefeater Gin is the only major premium gin distilled in the heart of the Capital. However, that's not the only thing that makes Beefeater Gin special.

This book tells the story of Beefeater Gin from the original recipe invented by entrepreneur James Burrough in the 1860s to its current renaissance under the ownership of Pernod Ricard. That story is also the story of the development of gin itself, the establishment of London as a major distilling centre for England's national spirit and how drinking culture has changed over time in London Dry Gin's birthplace.

Today, its heritage, quality and London provenance has made Beefeater Gin one of the world's most revered gins. But perhaps the most important reason why experts consider Beefeater the quintessential London Dry Gin is because of its taste. The bold, full-bodied flavour that James Burrough envisaged as the spirit of the Yeoman Warders at The Tower of London still comes through with every sip.

"BURROUGH'S
BEEFEATER"

INTERNATIONAL EXHIBITION.

LONDON 1873.

James Burrough

BEEFEATER BRAND.

ESTABLISHED 1820.

LONDON
OLD TOM GIN.

JAMES BURROUGH LTD. CALE DISTILLERY, LONDON. S.E. ENG.

EARLY HISTORY OF GIN

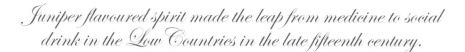

Juniper flavoured spirit made the leap from medicine to social drink in the Low Countries in the late fifteenth century.

The spirit we know as London Dry Gin most likely started life as a juniper flavoured medicinal potion produced by the Benedictine monks of Salerno in Italy in the eleventh century. These first apothecaries had rediscovered the writings of Greek and Arab scholars on distillation and made remedies using spirits distilled from wine together with different herbs, spices, berries and roots. Juniper berries were already prized as a cure for various kidney and bladder disorders, arthritis and gout. Later juniper took on almost magical properties, as it was believed to protect against the Black Death, the bubonic plague that stalked Europe throughout the Middle Ages. People not only consumed juniper, they wore masks filled with juniper berries to inhale its precious aromas.

Juniper flavoured spirit made the leap from medicine to social drink in the Low Countries in the late fifteenth century. The ever-inventive Dutch had perfected the art of distilling from grain to make an unsophisticated spirit they called brandewijn. Its malty, grainy flavour combined perfectly with juniper and other spices in a drink christened genever from the French word for juniper – *genièvre*. English soldiers and sailors fighting in the long European wars of the seventeenth century encountered genever as Dutch Courage, given as morale boosting tots before battle. When they returned home they brought this new drink with them. By 1650 London was also home to over 6000 Dutchmen and a hub of both the legal and smuggled genever trade. However, genever, or gin as it was now known, was still something of a secret as the English were not yet a nation of spirit drinkers.

The birth of English distilling. In seventeenth century England distilling of Aqua Vitae, Aqua Composita and other 'strong and hot waters' was still small scale, mostly confined to producing spirit for medicinal use and to supply drink for the King's ships and merchant navy for use on board and as trade goods. Distilling, however, was slowly growing in importance and in 1638 the Worshipful Company of Distillers was formally incorporated. The purpose of the Company was to control the distilling trade and oversee the practice of distilling in London.

Opposite: Distilling in the seventeenth century from John French's 'The Art of Distillation' 1667

THE DRINK DU JOUR

Drinking spirits was not only fashionable, it was a sign of patriotism and a desire to embrace the new.

Everything changed with the arrival of William of Orange on the British throne in 1688. The Glorious Revolution that resulted in the replacement of the Catholic Stewart King James II by his Dutch Protestant son-in-law was a turning point in English social history. One of its most immediate effects was to set in motion a chain of events that would transform virtually every aspect of English culture. It would also result in London becoming the epicentre of a great distilling industry whose vast energies were devoted to the production of England's own national spirit – gin.

One of the first pieces of legislation passed under William's reign was an Act to restrict imports of French wine and brandy and encourage the production of 'good and wholesome brandies, Aqua Vitae and spirits, drawn and made from malted corn'. From now on, almost anyone could take out a licence to distil. English distillers received a further boost when new taxes on beer in 1694 made spirits cheaper than beer for the first time. The deregulation of distilling coincided with the growing fashion for drinking gin made popular by the genever drinking habits of the new King and his Court. Drinking spirits was not only fashionable, it was a sign of patriotism and a desire to embrace the new. Overnight, gin became the people's darling.

Gin was first sold in earthenware crocks still used today for many brands of Dutch genéver. Later Dutch distillers developed an elongated heart shape glass bottle, which could be more easily transported in bulk. English distillers copied the style of these bottles. In the 1890s gin began to be sold in branded bottles and now clear glass was more often used as buyers in overseas markets wanted to see exactly what was in the bottle.

King William III and Queen Mary II. Queen Mary was the daughter of James II who had succeeded to the throne in 1685. James was unpopular because he was a Catholic. In 1688 he was deposed and the Crown offered to his Protestant daughter, Mary, who was married to her cousin, William of Orange. William and Mary ruled jointly until 1694 when Mary died. William continued to rule until his death in 1702. Because they had no heirs the Crown then passed to Mary's sister, Queen Anne.

Below: Portrait of King William III and Queen Mary II (engraving by unnamed artist)

MADAM GENEVA RULES

During the first half of the eighteenth century in London the birth rate was lower than the death rate, seventy-five percent of all children christened were buried before the age of five and there were two burials to every baptism.

By the beginning of the eighteenth century vast quantities of cheap gin were readily available, with disastrous consequences particularly in London. The slums of St. Giles, just behind what is now Oxford Street, were the centre of the Gin Craze as the urban poor, who weren't used to drinking spirits, discovered a new drink that would quickly get them drunk. This area was the setting for William Hogarth's famous engraving, 'Gin Lane' which graphically illustrates the effects of the gin mania that gripped the city. Here are arresting images of the drunken mother letting her child fall from her arms whilst desperate customers besiege the pawnbrokers and crowds storm the gin shop. This powerful piece of propaganda supported the shocking contemporary statistics above.

Records speak of the hospices and hospitals in the city packed with 'increasing multitudes of dropsical and consumptive people arising from the effects of spirituous liquors'.

Numerous pamphlets and magazine articles denounced gin as the ruin of family life. The demand for reform became unstoppable and many attempts were made to control the Gin Craze from the 1730s onwards. Nothing changed. By 1743 consumption had risen to the point where proportionately every man, woman and child in London was drinking over a litre of gin a week. In 1751 nine thousand children in London died of alcohol poisoning. In 1751 Parliament passed a law known as the Tippling Act, the first effective control of the production and sale of gin. It was followed by more legislation and a steady rise in excise duties designed to discourage the back street boys.

Gin Lane. The area of St. Giles pictured here stood roughly where Centrepoint is now. In the background is the spire of Nicholas Hawksmoor's St. George's Church in Bloomsbury, which has been recently restored. In the 18th century, the houses at St. Giles were called 'rookeries' because they consisted of houses and gardens that had been divided so much that people were packed into nests.

Around here there was a famous signboard over a gin shop that read: 'Drunk for a penny, dead drunk for tuppence, straw for free'. If you couldn't afford a glass of the spirit, you could buy a gin-soaked rag to suck. It was estimated that, by 1737, a quarter of the buildings in St. Giles were drinking dens.
Opposite: Gin Lane by William Hogarth, 1751

GIN LANE.

S. GRIPE PAWN BROKER

KILMAN DISTILLER

GIN ROYAL

Gin curſed Fiend, with Fury fraught,
Makes human Race a Prey.
It enters by a deadly Draught
And ſteals our Life away.

Virtue and Truth driv'n to Deſpair,
It's Rage compells to fly.
But cheriſhes with helliſh Care,
Theft, Murder, Perjury.

Damn'd Cup! that on the Vitals preys,
That liquid Fire contains,
Which Madneſs to the Heart conveys,
And rolls it thro' the Veins.

I   I

Death of Madam Geneva. The Gin Act of 1736 caused riots and unrest all over the country. The night before the Act became law, London's gin shops and taverns were draped in black and mock funeral processions carrying effigies of Madam Geneva, as gin was affectionately known, took place all over the city. One of the biggest funerals for Madam Geneva took place in Swallow Street behind Piccadilly.

Below: A Funeral Procession for Madame Geneva by unknown artist, 1751

Beer Street. London's brewers, anxious to regain their business, leaped on the anti-gin bandwagon. They denounced gin as foreign and poisonous whilst promoting beer as wholesome and English. The companion piece to Hogarth's 'Gin Lane' was 'Beer Street' where all was order and calm.

Opposite: Beer Street by William Hogarth, 1751

BEER STREET.

Beer, happy Produce of our Isle
Can sinewy Strength impart,
And wearied with Fatigue and Toil
Can chear each manly Heart.

Labour and Art upheld by Thee
Successfully advance,
We quaff Thy balmy Juice with Glee
And Water leave to France.

Genius of Health, thy grateful Taste
Rivals the Cup of Jove,
And warms each English generous Breast
With Liberty and Love.

Design'd by W. Hogarth.   Publish'd according to Act of Parliament Feb.y 1. 1751.   Price 1.s

THE BIRTH OF AN INDUSTRY

By the end of the eighteenth century cheap gin was no more. Strict controls led to the proper supervision and management of distilling which now became a respectable business.

London was the centre of the gin trade and, in 1790, was producing 90% of English gin. London was the natural home for this fledgling industry thanks to the River Thames, the motorway of its time. Via the river, goods could be brought from the sea into the heart of the city and London's distillers had easy access to the raw ingredients they needed: precious cargoes of oranges, lemons, spices and herbs landing on docks and quays along the Thames; sugar from British colonies in the Caribbean; grain brought in from the surrounding countryside.

In 1794 there were over 40 distillers, malt distillers and rectifiers in the Cities of London and Westminster and the Borough of Southwark. Once regulation and taxation took effect, many small players soon disappeared but some familiar names from that time – Booth, Gordon, Burnett and Boords – are still around. They were joined later by companies like Tanqueray and Gilbey. These successful businesses located in those parts of London that were not only convenient for the Thames but also close to sources of pure water. And they thrived.

With the reorganisation of the drinks industry in the 1970s, many distillers moved out of London. Today only one great distilling house remains in the capital and that is the House of James Burrough, makers of Beefeater, the finest London Dry Gin.

London's dockyards. In the 18th century, when gin distilling was becoming established as one of London's most important industries, London's dockyards doubled in size and expanded eastwards to accommodate more and bigger vessels. Then London had the biggest and busiest port in the world, was the biggest and richest city in the world and had one of the world's biggest urban populations. All thanks to Father Thames.

Opposite: The Rhinebeck Panorama of London, Panel 2, c.1810

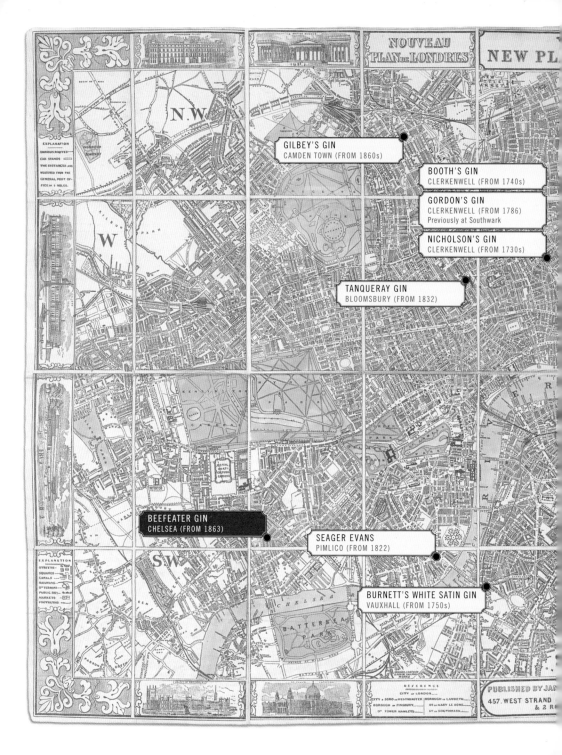

NOUVEAU PLAN DE LONDRES

NEW PL

N.W.

W

S.W.

GILBEY'S GIN
CAMDEN TOWN (FROM 1860s)

BOOTH'S GIN
CLERKENWELL (FROM 1740s)

GORDON'S GIN
CLERKENWELL (FROM 1786)
Previously at Southwark

NICHOLSON'S GIN
CLERKENWELL (FROM 1730s)

TANQUERAY GIN
BLOOMSBURY (FROM 1832)

BEEFEATER GIN
CHELSEA (FROM 1863)

SEAGER EVANS
PIMLICO (FROM 1822)

BURNETT'S WHITE SATIN GIN
VAUXHALL (FROM 1750s)

PUBLISHED BY JA
457. WEST STRAND
& 2 R

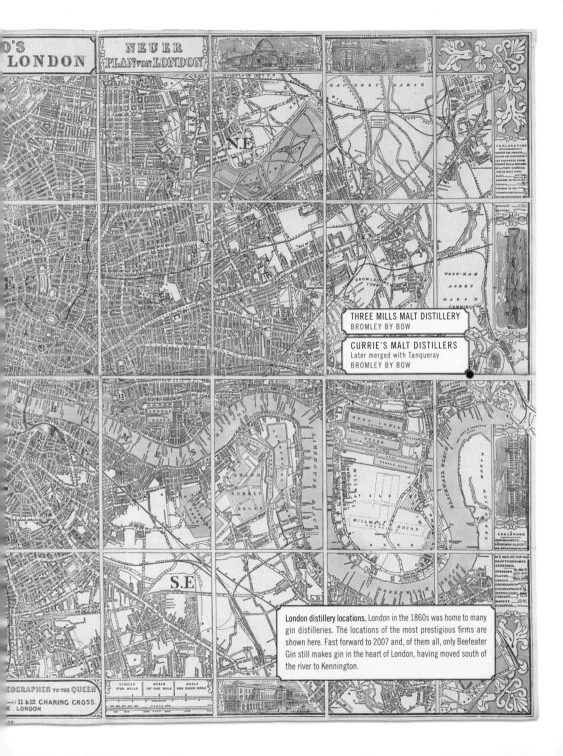

N.E

THREE MILLS MALT DISTILLERY
BROMLEY BY BOW

CURRIE'S MALT DISTILLERS
Later merged with Tanqueray
BROMLEY BY BOW

S.E

London distillery locations. London in the 1860s was home to many gin distilleries. The locations of the most prestigious firms are shown here. Fast forward to 2007 and, of them all, only Beefeater Gin still makes gin in the heart of London, having moved south of the river to Kennington.

ECHELLE D'UN MILLE   SCALE OF ONE MILE   SKALF VON EINER MEILE

THE UNSTOPPABLE RISE OF LONDON DRY

Originally called 'Dry Gin' to distinguish it from sweet gin, it came to be known as 'London Dry' because most of the distillers making this style of gin were based in London.

The gin that fuelled London's Gin Craze was known as Old Tom. Heavily sweetened with sugar and glycerine and strongly flavoured with juniper and other herbs to conceal off flavours, it resembled modern day Dutch oude genever. This style prevailed until the 1830s when the invention of the continuous still meant that a lighter, cleaner base spirit could be made cost effectively. So, instead of disguising the flavour of rough spirit with sugar and strong spices, this pure spirit could be gently enhanced by redistilling with subtler botanical flavourings. Originally called 'Dry Gin' to distinguish it from sweet gin, it came to be known as 'London Dry' because most of the distillers making this style of gin were based in London.

This more sophisticated spirit attracted new consumers far removed from London's slum dwellers. Middle class women bought their gin in grocery shops thanks to a law of 1872 that allowed shops to retail spirits. They called it 'white wine'. The suspension of excise duties on gin for export in 1850 opened up new markets for London gin. It travelled all over the world helped by the fondness of the Royal Navy for gin particularly when mixed with the newly invented Rose's Lime Juice to prevent scurvy. Wherever the Navy went, gin went too. In far-flung corners of the Empire expats drank their London Dry Gin with another new invention – tonic water. Gin's unstoppable rise to respectability was further assisted by the arrival of Gin Palaces in Victorian times. They were richly ornate oases of glamour and comfort compared with the makeshift drinking dens of former days. In the 1850s there were at least five thousand in London and they played a major role in introducing the idea of drink as a social pleasure, no longer a short-cut to oblivion.

By the beginning of the 20th century London Dry Gin became the predominant gin style although many distillers, including James Burrough Limited, made Old Tom Gin until well into the 1950s.

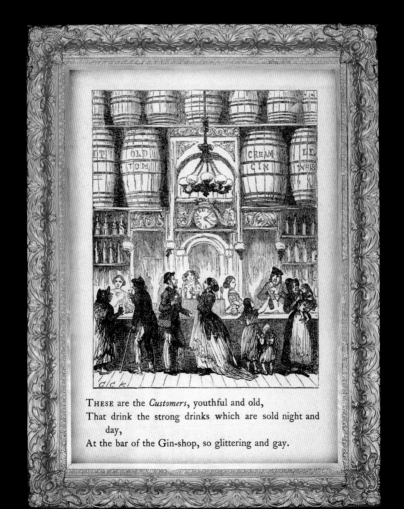

THESE are the *Customers*, youthful and old,
That drink the strong drinks which are sold night and
day,
At the bar of the Gin-shop, so glittering and gay.

JAMES BURROUGH, THE FIRST MIXOLOGIST

Like those pioneering distillers, the Salerno monks,
Burrough used his medical knowledge to
perfect and refine his recipes.

James Burrough, the founder of Beefeater Gin, was an enterprising character. Born in Ottery St. Mary in Devon in 1835, he trained as a pharmacist in Exeter before setting off to seek his fortune in North America. In 1855 he went into partnership in a Toronto chemists' business, Bentley & Burrough. Five years later, James returned to the UK in search of his next commercial opportunity. That was the Chelsea distilling and rectifying firm of John Taylor dating back to 1820, which James bought for £400 in 1863.

Taylor's specialised in the production of liqueurs – cherry brandy, Curaçao, orange bitters, maraschino, noyeau and others. The Distillery also produced fruit gins and punches. It had an excellent reputation and loyal customers such as Fortnum & Mason. James took over the business lock, stock and barrel, renaming it 'James Burrough, Distiller and Importer of Foreign Liqueurs'. Using many of the firm's existing suppliers he continued to source the different fruits, French brandy, liqueurs and the other spirits he needed to make his products. Above all James constantly experimented. He had an inquiring mind. Like those pioneering distillers, the Salerno monks, he used his pharmaceutical knowledge to perfect and refine his recipes, now in a relentless drive for purity and quality. The business did well and in 1871 James began to improve and extend the Distillery buildings.

This house in Marlborough Square, close to Chelsea green, was the home of the Burrough family – James, his wife Emma, and their six children. James Burrough's diary of 1863 notes that he took possession of the house on the 10th March, the same day he got married. The Burroughs finally bought the property in 1898. The Distillery was in Cale Street immediately to the rear of this house. As the business grew the family home also housed the company offices.

As these extracts from his notebooks demonstrate, James Burrough had an inquiring mind. He had long experimented with recipes for household products such as toothpaste, furniture polishes and incense. He had also devised his own formulae for various different types of pharmaceutical remedies. Soon he turned his attention to alcoholic drinks and his first recipe for blackcurrant gin is dated 1849. Once James acquired the Distillery in Chelsea in 1863 his notebooks were filled with different recipes for liqueurs, cordials and other spirits as well as information on how to improve the distilling process.

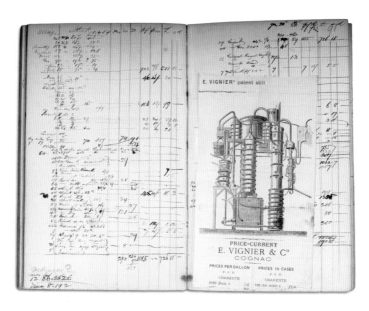

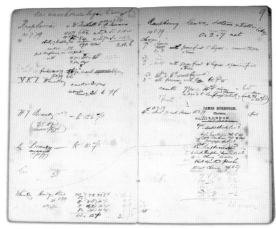

THE BIRTH OF AN ICONIC BRAND

Beefeater Gin met with instant success and rapidly became the James Burrough Company's flagship product.

The main focus of James Burrough's Chelsea Distillery remained the production of liqueurs and cordials made from imported brandies and natural flavourings. By 1876 it was a different story. The phylloxera plague had almost destroyed French vineyards and brandy was virtually unobtainable. In common with other London distillers and rectifiers, James now had to source spirits from nearer home. Entrepreneurial as ever, he had begun buying whisky from Scotland as well as large quantities of Irish whiskey. He bottled these under various upmarket names such as Old Hermit and Ozone and promoted them as 'British liqueurs', a standard practice designed to make whisky seem more sophisticated. At the same time James turned his attention to the other domestic spirit that would benefit enormously from the brandy shortage – English gin.

From 1876 onwards the company's stock lists feature an ever increasing portfolio of gins under brand names such as Ye Old Chelsey, Black Cat Gin, James Burrough London Dry and Old Tom Gins and even an aged Fine Old Malt Gin. Then comes the first appearance of Beefeater Gin, named after the Beefeaters at the Tower of London who play such a prominent role in the rich pageantry and tradition of London life. Beefeater Gin met with instant success and rapidly became the James Burrough Company's flagship product.

James Burrough's use of 'Beefeater' as the name for his flagship brand was revolutionary. Instead of choosing a family or location name like other gin brands, he chose an aspirational image that would position his brand as the ultimate London Dry Gin.

In James' quest to make the perfect gin it's likely that he tried out different combinations of the ingredients he was familiar with. The earliest invoices on file at the Distillery record his purchases of Seville oranges from a Mrs Isaacs at the fruit market in Covent Garden. He would have needed good quality oranges to make the orange-based Curaçao, and orange bitters, two of his biggest sellers. Certainly he would have quickly learned their flavour potential in distillation and his recipe book from 1879 shows him using a bigger proportion of orange in his gin recipe than is usual. So perhaps Beefeater's unique citrus character can be traced to James Burrough's innate love of experimentation, the proven success of his existing orange flavoured products and the fact that he had found an excellent supplier on whom he could depend.

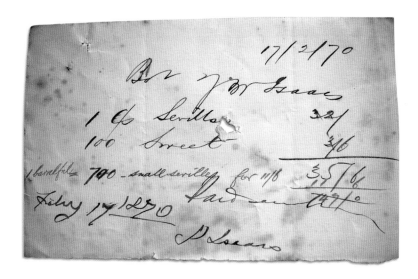

Below: The James Burrough price list of 1909 contains a large range of fruit gins – sloe, blackberry, cherry, damson, ginger, lemon, orange and rue amongst them. Over time that list was gradually whittled down as fruit gins and liqueurs went out of fashion. In the 1970s all liqueur and fruit gin production stopped because the capacity was required for white spirits.

Below: The first recorded licence for the Distillery in Cale Street, Chelsea is dated 1829. At that time John Taylor owned the company. A licence cost £10 and had to be renewed annually.

Above: James Burrough Ltd. had a list of prestigious clients that included Hedges & Butler, Fortnum & Mason and other well known retailers, many of whom are still around today.

Opposite: An early price list shows the diversity of bottles and containers used for the company's gin, liqueurs and bottled fruit. These ceramic bottles were specially commissioned.

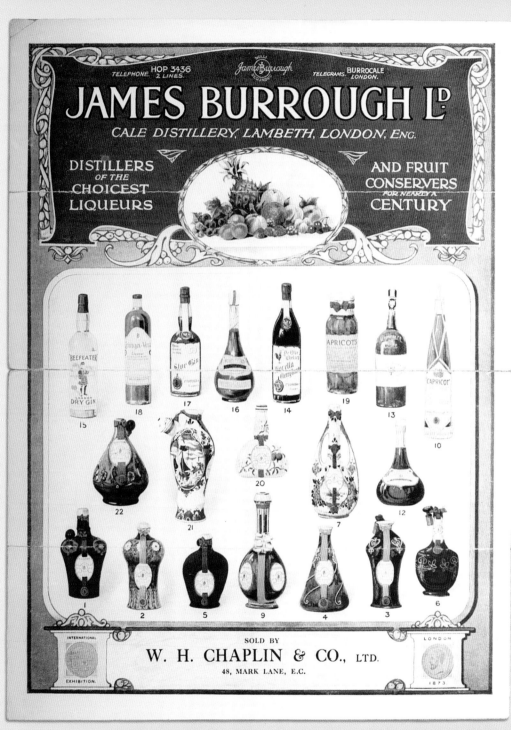

A FAMILY BUSINESS

⚬⚬⚬

In 1897 James Burrough died, handing over the business to his sons Frederick and Ernest.

In 1906, with only two years to run on the lease in Chelsea, the Burrough family began the move across the river to Lambeth. A distillery was purchased at 26 Hutton Road and a major programme of refurbishment and rebuilding took place. They invested in the latest equipment including a new still from J Dore & Sons (successors to the famous Aeneas Coffey who had invented the continuous still) in order to expand production. James Burrough Ltd. moved to the new distillery in 1908. It was renamed the Cale Distillery to preserve the name of the original premises in Cale Street in Chelsea.

Lambeth was an area that was popular with brewers and distillers because of its proximity to the River Thames and the much vaunted purity of its wells. There was, indeed probably still is, a famous spring of clear water on the road to Wandsworth, called Vauxhall Well, dating back to the Middle Ages. It was said never to freeze, even in the coldest winters.

The Burrough company prospered in its new location. Production of gin and liqueurs increased but now with a major emphasis on the company's premium product, the 'Finest London Distilled Beefeater Gin' that was available in both the London Dry and Old Tom styles. In 1911 Beefeater Gin was awarded the prestigious Gold Medal at the Festival of Empire Imperial Exhibition at Crystal Palace in London. In 1921 the company expanded further and opened its own bonded warehouses in Camberwell, which were equipped with modern bottling and blending machinery.

These salt glaze stoneware pocket flasks – known as 'flat bottles' – were produced in London potteries between 1800 and 1850 and were used to carry gin. Lambeth was famous for its potteries which once stretched along the riverside from Westminster Bridge to Vauxhall. The well-known Royal Doulton Pottery had several premises in Lambeth close to Beefeater's Cale Distillery.

Top: This picture of the James Burrough stand at the Brewers Exhibition of 1925 shows how much emphasis is now being given to the promotion of Beefeater Gin with strong branding of the company as 'Distillers of Beefeater Gin and Liqueurs'.

Bottom: The Cale Distillery at Hutton Road. At Hutton Road there was a well beneath the Distillery to supply water. In its heyday the Distillery had what was believed to be the largest rectifying still of any gin distillery in the UK. The bottling hall (pictured bottom right) was the most advanced of its time.

THE BIGGEST EXPORT GIN IN THE WORLD

Cocktails for Hitler.

Like many other distillers in the UK, James Burrough suffered badly during the Second World War. Grain was rationed because it was needed for food and distilling was restricted, so most alcohol production was diverted to the war effort, a policy described by the stoical British as "Cocktails for Hitler". After the War, whilst it was relatively simple to recommence gin distilling (unlike whisky which had to be aged), there were other problems.

Before the War, Beefeater had established a very successful export business. 1906 saw the first reference to the USA as a market for Beefeater Gin and soon it was being exported to Greece, France, Egypt, China, Canada, India, New Zealand, Australia, Malta, Spain and South Africa. Much of this valuable trade was lost during the War but, once again, the energy and vision of the Burrough family came to the rescue. Under the leadership of the third generation, Eric, Alan and Norman Burrough, and Neville Hayman (the husband of James' granddaughter), the company focused relentlessly on the drive to build export markets for Beefeater Gin. Eric Burrough led this crusade, crisscrossing the world several times over in the quest for overseas distribution. His efforts soon paid off. In 1956 shipments of Beefeater to the US reached record levels. By the next year over 65% of Beefeater production was exported.

Demand soon outstripped supply and the Hutton Road Distillery could no longer cope with production. In 1958 the company moved to its present home in Montford Place in Kennington where, on a site once occupied by the Haywards Military Pickle factory, a new distillery was built. With the increased capacity Beefeater Gin went from strength to strength. It became the biggest export gin brand in the world and in 1963 Beefeater accounted for three out of every four bottles of gin imported into the US. In 1965 another still house was built at the new distillery to cater for the ever expanding demand. Today Beefeater Gin is the No. 1 imported gin in Spain and the No. 3 in the US – the world's two largest premium gin markets.

In 1987 James Burrough was purchased by Whitbread and ceased to be a family business. In 1989 Beefeater Gin passed into the ownership of Allied Lyons which later became Allied Domecq Spirits and Wine. Pernod Ricard acquired the majority of the Allied Domecq portfolio in 2005. Beefeater Gin is now in a stable of prestigious spirit brands that include Chivas Regal and Ballantine's whiskies, Martell Cognac and Havana Club rums.

Baroness Phillips presents Norman Burrough with the Queen's Award. The Queen's Award for Enterprise is awarded to British companies who excel at international trade, innovation or sustainable development. The prestigious award is the greatest accolade a British company can receive and it has been won five times by Beefeater Gin in 1966, 1969, 1971, 1976 and 1985.

The signing of an agreement with Rudy Kopf of Kobrand to distribute Beefeater Gin in the US was one of Eric Burrough's most important achievements. Sales exploded and in 1961 the company presented Rudy with a Rolls Royce to mark their gratitude. By 1969 shipments of Beefeater Gin via Kobrand had reached over one million cases.

The Beefeater Club was founded in 1938 to promote Beefeater Gin and provide support to worthy charities who benefited from members' annual subscriptions. Members paid a modest joining fee and in return received their insignia – a tie for the men, a brooch for the ladies. There were only 2 rules: To specify Beefeater when asking for gin and to wear their insignia on a Friday.

On the maiden voyage of the QE2 to New York in 1969 Beefeater Gin was the only gin aboard. The US was a huge market for Beefeater Gin and, in 1980, it broke through the two million case barrier.

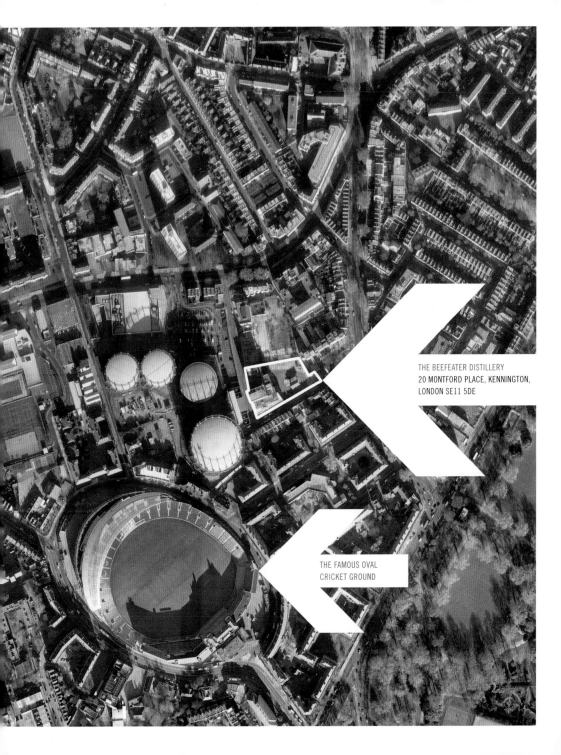

THE BEEFEATER DISTILLERY
20 MONTFORD PLACE, KENNINGTON,
LONDON SE11 5DE

THE FAMOUS OVAL
CRICKET GROUND

THE NAME KENNINGTON WAS DERIVED FROM THE OLD SAXON WORD – KYNING-TUN – MEANING THE PLACE OR TOWN OF THE KING. IT HAD MANY ROYAL CONNECTIONS AND STILL DOES. THE MANOR OF KENNINGTON WAS ONCE OWNED BY RICHARD THE LION HEART AND THE FAMOUS OVAL CRICKET GROUND, ONCE A CABBAGE GARDEN, IS BUILT ON LAND THAT BELONGS TO THE PRINCE OF WALES. OVER CENTURIES KENNINGTON HAS ALSO BEEN HOME TO MANY FAMOUS LONDONERS INCLUDING GEOFFREY CHAUCER, WILLIAM HOGARTH, CHARLIE CHAPLIN AND, OF COURSE, THE KING OF GINS: BEEFEATER GIN.

BEEFEATER PEOPLE

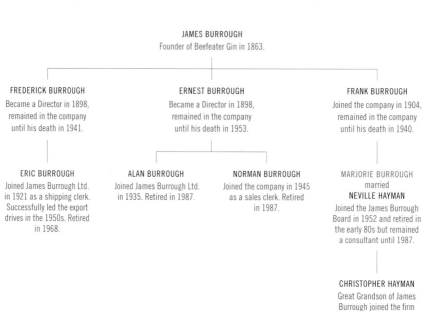

Beefeater people tend to stay at Beefeater.

In June 1898 the first Meeting of the Board of James Burrough Ltd. took place. In attendance were Frederick and Ernest Burrough, George William Browne and Thomas Tedbury, the Company's first Chairman. For years the company remained very much a family affair, with the directors meeting for a drink in the tasting room at eleven each morning in lieu of formal proceedings.

JAMES BURROUGH
Founder of Beefeater Gin in 1863.

FREDERICK BURROUGH
Became a Director in 1898, remained in the company until his death in 1941.

ERNEST BURROUGH
Became a Director in 1898, remained in the company until his death in 1953.

FRANK BURROUGH
Joined the company in 1904, remained in the company until his death in 1940.

ERIC BURROUGH
Joined James Burrough Ltd. in 1921 as a shipping clerk. Successfully led the export drives in the 1950s. Retired in 1968.

ALAN BURROUGH
Joined James Burrough Ltd. in 1935. Retired in 1987.

NORMAN BURROUGH
Joined the company in 1945 as a sales clerk. Retired in 1987.

MARJORIE BURROUGH
married
NEVILLE HAYMAN
Joined the James Burrough Board in 1952 and retired in the early 80s but remained a consultant until 1987.

CHRISTOPHER HAYMAN
Great Grandson of James Burrough joined the firm in the 1970s, became Operations Director in 1977. Left in 1987 when James Burrough was acquired by Whitbread.

James Burrough

Frederick Burrough

Ernest Burrough

Frank Burrough

Eric Burrough

Alan Burrough

Norman Burrough

Neville Hayman

Christopher Hayman

Beefeater people tend to stay at Beefeater. That is as true today as it was when James Burrough was family owned. As these pictures show, Beefeater had a strong family ethos and a loyal and dedicated staff. The annual staff outing was the highlight of the year. The tradition began in the earliest days of the company and involved everyone from the Chairman down embarking for a day out, often to the seaside. A splendid lunch and tea would be followed by drinks, dancing and entertainment until late. Then everyone was taken home by coach.

Brian Martin (Beefeater Head Distiller 1955-95) joined James Burrough Ltd. in 1955 and rose through the company to become Head Distiller. On his watch the company moved from Hutton Road to Montford Place and Beefeater Gin became the best selling premium gin in the world.

Desmond Payne (Beefeater Master Distiller since 1995) knows more about making premium gin than anyone else. He is in charge of preserving the integrity of Beefeater Gin's recipe and is personally involved with every aspect of Beefeater production from selecting the botanicals to supervising the distillation process.

THE BEEFEATERS, A SYMBOL OF LONDON

*The Yeoman Warders are still
Her Majesty the Queen's official bodyguards
and attend her on all major state occasions.*

Beefeater Gin is named after the Guards at the Tower of London. Whether dressed in their everyday red and blue tunics or in their dazzling state uniforms of scarlet and gold, they are as much a symbol of London as Big Ben and the famous red buses. Established by King Henry VIII in 1485 as his personal bodyguards, their official title is 'Yeoman Warders of Her Majesty's Royal Palace and Fortress the Tower of London and Members of the Sovereign's Body Guard of the Yeoman Guard Extraordinary'. The Beefeater nickname most likely arose from the fact that they enjoyed special dietary privileges. At a time when meat was a luxury, history records that the Beefeaters shared 18lb of mutton, 16lb of veal, and 24lb of beef as a daily ration! Another possible explanation for the name is that it is derived from the French word for the guards at the French palaces: *buffetiers*.

The Yeoman Warders are still Her Majesty the Queen's official bodyguards and attend her on all major state occasions. They also act as guides showing visitors around the Tower's treasures. Beefeater Gin has always maintained close links with the Beefeaters, entertaining them every year with a Christmas lunch at the Distillery and, in return, being invited to the Tower to watch the Ceremony of the Keys. In addition all Beefeaters receive a very welcome bottle of Beefeater Gin on their birthdays.

The Beefeater on the Beefeater bottle wears the ceremonial uniform that is still used on all important state occasions. It consists of a scarlet tunic, scarlet breeches and stockings and a round hat called a Tudor bonnet. Queen Elizabeth I introduced the distinctive white ruff. The heavily embroidered tunic (detail shown opposite) includes emblems of the thistle, rose and shamrock, the national symbols of Scotland, England and Ireland. The initials VR stand for Victoria Regina (Latin for queen). Modern uniforms bear the initials ER for Elizabeth Regina representing the present Queen Elizabeth II.

The Ravens. One of the most important of the Beefeaters' duties at the Tower of London is to look after the seven resident ravens. Legend has it that, should the ravens ever leave, both the Tower and the Monarchy will fall.

The Tower of London. William the Conqueror began to build the Tower of London in 1085. Over its 900 year history the Tower has been a fortress, royal palace and a prison, a place where traitors were executed, an armoury, a treasury, a mint and even a zoo.

HOW BEEFEATER GIN IS MADE

*No other gin is made like Beefeater and
no other gin tastes like Beefeater.*

Every drop of Beefeater London Dry Gin is still made in the heart of London at the Kennington Distillery. That's not the only thing that differentiates Beefeater from other London Dry Gins. Beefeater Gin is a handcrafted gin, made in a unique way by a dedicated team under the supervision of Master Distiller, Desmond Payne.

The process starts with charging copper pot stills with high quality neutral grain spirit from the nearby Greenwich Distillery. Then nine carefully selected natural botanicals are added in the exact proportions specified by James Burrough. Spirit and botanicals are left to steep in the still for a full 24 hours. This long, slow process allows for both a fuller extraction of flavour from the botanicals and the capture of a wider range of the more volatile oils, resulting in a more complex gin.

After steeping, the stills are gently heated and the botanical infused spirit begins its journey from liquid to vapour before returning to liquid, now gin. Gin distillation is a mysterious process and each botanical releases its flavour at different stages, so the speed at which the still is run is crucial. Too fast and the flavour profile is diluted. Too slow and unwanted elements of the spirit are picked up. Deciding when to make the 'middle cut' as it is called is a very important task for the Distiller. He samples the liquid coming through the spirit safe until he is satisfied that it has the flavours and characteristics he wants. This, the heart of Beefeater Gin, is collected.

The final stage of production is to reduce the gin to its bottling strength with pure softened water. Unlike other distillers we have always maintained the alcoholic strength of our gin at 40% abv or above. At this strength the complex bands of flavour and more volatile citrus elements within Beefeater Gin are held in perfect balance. The insistence on pure water dates back to the time when all the principal gin distilleries were located in parts of London that were noted for the quality of their water.

The new still house at the Beefeater Distillery completed in 1966.

THE DISTILLATION PROCESS

NEUTRAL SPIRIT

STILL

BOTANICALS

01

STEEPING: 24 HOURS

Beefeater Gin's botanicals are steeped for 24 hours – longer than any other premium gin – to create a full-flavoured and perfectly balanced gin.

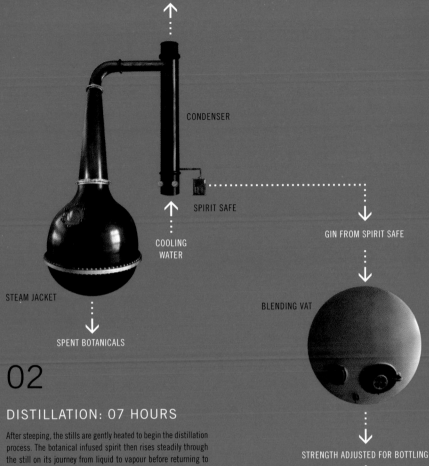

CONDENSER

SPIRIT SAFE

COOLING
WATER

GIN FROM SPIRIT SAFE

STEAM JACKET

BLENDING VAT

SPENT BOTANICALS

02

DISTILLATION: 07 HOURS

After steeping, the stills are gently heated to begin the distillation process. The botanical infused spirit then rises steadily through the still on its journey from liquid to vapour before returning to liquid, now gin, as it cools.

MAKING THE CUT

As the gin travels through the spirit safe it is constantly monitored by the stillman. Only the middle cut (called the heart) is collected for Beefeater Gin and the rest is separated as a by-product. This part of the distillation process is called 'making the cut'.

STRENGTH ADJUSTED FOR BOTTLING

03

BOTTLING

The final stage of production is to reduce the strength of Beefeater Gin to its bottling strength. We do this by adding pure, softened water to the spirit.

THE BOTANICALS

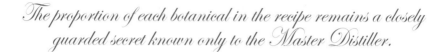

The proportion of each botanical in the recipe remains a closely guarded secret known only to the Master Distiller.

The unique Beefeater recipe has changed little since the days of James Burrough. Beefeater's crisp, clean, well balanced flavour is still derived from 100% natural ingredients, known as the botanicals, brought to the London Distillery from all over the world. The principal botanicals in Beefeater Gin are juniper, coriander and the citrus peels that provide freshness and lift. The other botanicals in the recipe add complexity and depth.

JUNIPER

The best juniper grows wild on mountain slopes in Italy and Macedonia. Crops vary from year to year so, every September, the Master Distiller samples the harvest to create the exact blend of berries he requires. In Beefeater Gin the distinctive oily, piney taste of juniper is the palette on which is layered the subtle flavours of all the other botanicals in the recipe.

CORIANDER SEED

Coriander seeds are the second most important botanical in gin. The most highly flavoured coriander comes from Romania, Russia and Bulgaria. When distilled with the other botanicals, coriander seeds release ginger, sage and lemon flavours. These combine perfectly with the strong citrus elements of Beefeater Gin to produce a spiciness and freshness that linger in the mouth. Coriander also contributes to Beefeater's much vaunted dry peppery finish.

LEMON PEEL

The crisp, sharp flavours of Spanish lemons add another dimension to Beefeater's strong citrus profile. Only the peels are used and they are dried in the sun to enhance their rich oiliness.

SEVILLE ORANGE PEEL

Original recipe books at the Distillery in James Burrough's hand demonstrate his use of orange peel as a major botanical in his gin recipe. Ever since then, Beefeater Gin has had a more citrus character than other gins. Seville oranges, commonly found in marmalade, impart the fresh, clean, citrus notes that make Beefeater Gin instantly recognisable.

clockwise:

Juniper
Coriander seed
Lemon peel
Seville orange peel

ALMOND

Bitter almonds, ground to release their oil, are an essential part of the Beefeater botanicals profile. Almond brings a hint of marzipan and nuttiness whilst at the same time adding to Beefeater's complexity.

ANGELICA ROOT

The earthiness of angelica root from Flanders in Belgium is what makes Dry Gin dry. In Beefeater its woody, spicy notes also contribute to creating a complex yet integrated botanicals profile where, clustered around the distinctive keynote of juniper, no single aromatic overpowers.

ANGELICA SEED

Long ago the art of distilling was closely related to that of alchemy. As with alchemical processes, balance and harmony are all important when making gin. In Beefeater Gin angelica seeds impart fragrant, hop-like notes with a floral character, a counterpoint to the muskiness of angelica root.

LIQUORICE

The liquorice in Beefeater Gin comes from China. It contains natural sugars, bitter compounds, and a substance that produces the characteristic woody, bittersweet flavour, all of which are crucial to the underlying spiciness and mellowness of Beefeater Gin. Liquorice also softens and rounds out gin's mouthfeel.

ORRIS ROOT

In Beefeater Gin ground orris root from Italy is an essential part of the botanicals mix. Aromatic and floral in itself with a hint of Parma Violet, orris also holds the volatile elements of the other botanicals together and allows their subtle flavours to slowly and gently build.

clockwise:

Almond
Angelica root
Angelica seed
Liquorice
Orris root

FOCUSED ON QUALITY AND HERITAGE

A name that would capture the spirit of the world's greatest city and evoke images of strength and permanence.

James Burrough chose the name of his gin carefully. He wanted a name that people would remember, that would also capture the spirit of the world's greatest city and evoke images of strength and permanence. The first distinctive Beefeater bottle design encapsulated James' vision in the striking image of the Yeoman Warder. Later, one of the secrets of the success of Eric Burrough's export drive was that he emphasised the Beefeater branding to capitalise on the mania for everything British in the US following the Coronation of Queen Elizabeth II in 1953. By the 1960s Beefeater in the US was seen as a sign of Britain abroad. Over time, the design of Beefeater's promotional and advertising materials has evolved, but great care has always been taken to remain focused on the brand's exceptional quality.

Right from the start, the design of the Beefeater bottle has carried details of its prestigious medals and prizes. The quality of James Burrough's gin was first recognised at the International Exhibition of 1873 when it received the coveted Gold Medal. Ever since, Beefeater Gin has won more awards than other gin and is consistently placed in the top three at the world's most prestigious spirit competitions.

BURROUGH'S
BEEFEATER
DISTILLED
LONDON DRY GIN

The colourful Beefeater illustrated on the label is a representative of that corps of men originally formed by King Henry VII of England in 1485 to act as bodyguard, and as such they have always taken a leading place in officiating at Royal Ceremonies and State Banquets.

Beefeaters, in their picturesque uniform, have a world-wide reputation. The Tower of London, which is their official residence, remains the place beyond all others, except Windsor, where the local colour of every age in English history lingers. Outside these walls the Beefeaters may, perhaps, now be less well-known than in previous ages, but they are plainly the "Warders" of the Tower of London, faithful to Tudor masters. At eleven each night the Ceremony of the keys, when their royal ownership is challenged and declared, brings back the memory of many monarchs, and relates especially to the epoch when the Pretenders threatened the English throne. The Beefeaters remain always an emblem of all that is stately and distinguished in quality and style.

Since 1820 Burrough's Beefeater Gin has been the acknowledged peer of the world's finest gin. Like the Beefeater of tradition, Burrough's Beefeater Gin is of unique character—the best quality and of distinctive style. Its inimitable softness, combined with delicate flavour, makes for light and refreshing long drinks and for exceptional cocktails.

DISITRIBUTORS FOR EGYPT
MACDONALD & CO
ALEXANDRIA · CAIRO · PORT SAID

↘

BEEFEATER GIN'S ADVERTISING HAS ALWAYS BEEN AIMED AT THE DISCRIMINATING AND STYLE CONSCIOUS, USING VERY BRITISH HUMOUR AND STRIKING IMAGES TO CONVEY CORE VALUES OF QUALITY AND SOPHISTICATION. THE NEW 'FOREVER LONDON' ADVERTISING CAMPAIGN IS A DISTILLATION OF ALL THAT HAS GONE BEFORE. IT CEMENTS THE BRAND'S LONG ASSOCIATION WITH LONDON, ITS BIRTHPLACE, THROUGH QUIRKY AND IMPACTFUL VISUAL COLLAGES THAT ENCAPSULATE BOTH BEEFEATER'S TRADITIONAL HERITAGE AND ITS PLACE AT THE HEART OF CONTEMPORARY LONDON.

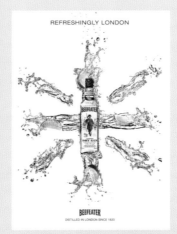

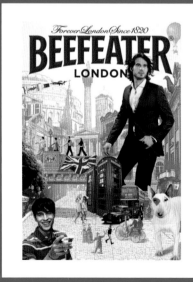

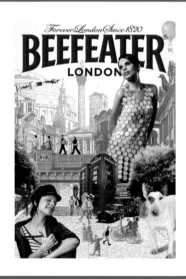

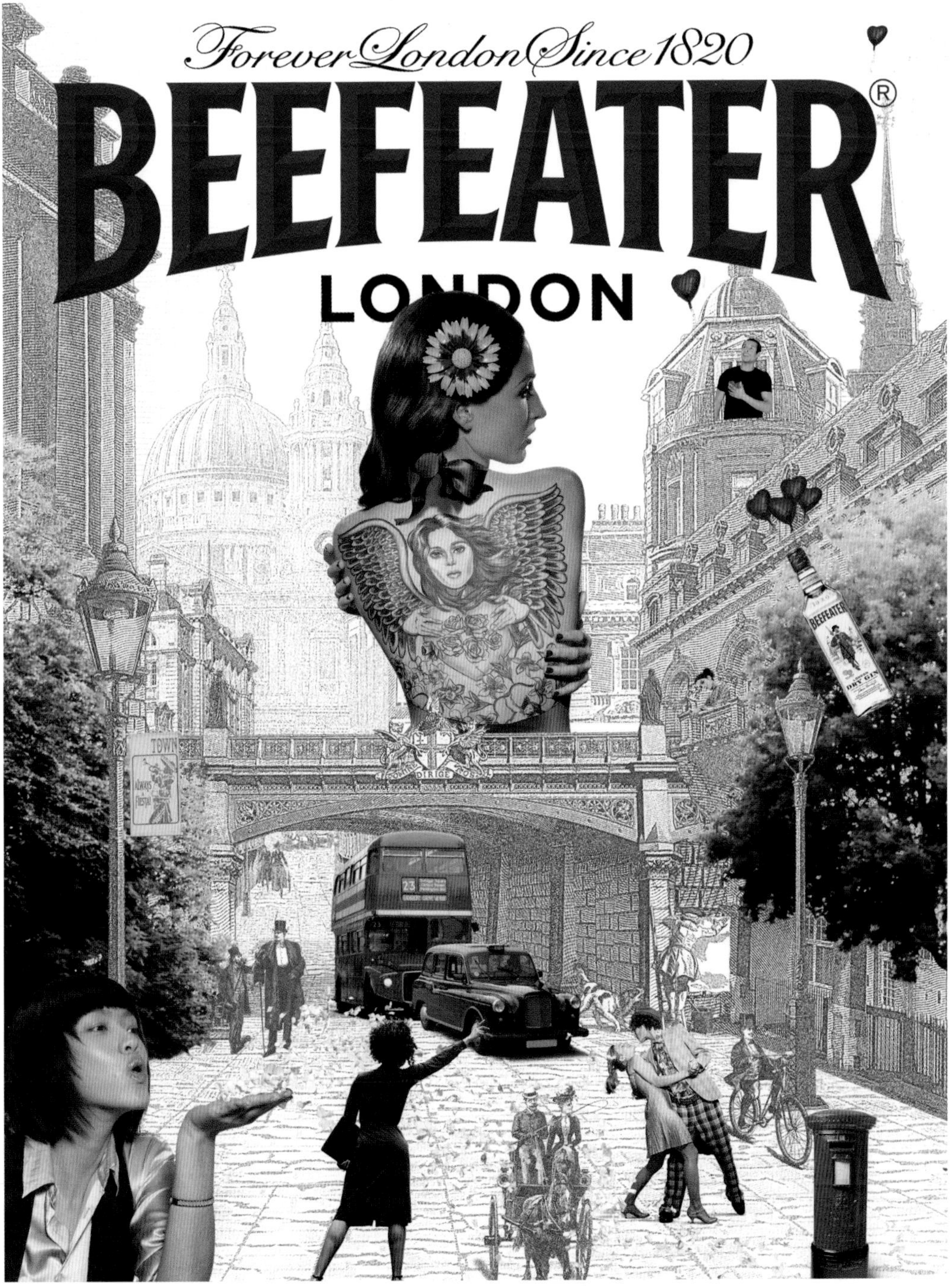

Beefeater advertising campaign launched in January 2007.

CLASSIC BEEFEATER COCKTAILS

Cocktails first arrived in London in the 1860s, brought over by sophisticated American travellers who imported the fashion for the sweet mixed drinks that were all the rage at home.

Many of these earliest cocktails were made from gin such as the Dog's Nose, a weird and wonderful combination of hot porter, gin, sugar and nutmeg.

Soon, American style cocktail bars could be found in the smartest hotels throughout the city. The first one was the Criterion in Piccadilly, which opened in the 1870s. Cocktails were drunk at home too in the cups, punches, toddies, flips, fizzes and slings of Victorian England. Many used the new style Dry Gin as their base and established it as a fashionable drink: a trend confirmed when Mrs. Beeton, an English icon, published a recipe for Gin Sling in her famous book.

In the 1920s London saw a new cocktail wave as many of America's leading barmen arrived in search of work, driven from home by Prohibition. Tastes by now had changed and gin cocktails were less sweet, more balanced and more aromatic. This new type of cocktail required robust, full-flavoured gin to carry complex flavours, which is why Beefeater met with such success. Then, as now, Beefeater Gin was the preferred choice for classic cocktails such as the Dry Martini, the Negroni and the White Lady.

NO ONE KNOWS WHERE THE WORD COCKTAIL COMES FROM!
There are a variety of explanations, one describing it as coming from the name Xochitl, an Aztec princess,
another from the description of a horse of mixed breeds. The most likely is that it comes from
the French word 'coquetel' meaning a mixed drink.

DRY MARTINI

In a large mixing glass three quarters filled with ice cubes pour:

3 shots Beefeater Gin
1 shot French dry vermouth
2 dashes orange bitters (optional)

Stir until ice cold. Strain liquid into a chilled martini glass. Garnish with a thin twist of lemon peel and drink immediately.

NEGRONI

1 shot Beefeater Gin
1 shot Campari
1 shot Italian sweet vermouth

Pour all ingredients into an ice filled tumbler and stir. Garnish with a large twist of orange peel.

WHITE LADY

2 shots Beefeater Gin
3/4 shot of orange Curaçao
3/4 shot freshly squeezed lemon juice
1/4 shot of sugar syrup
1 egg white

Shake with ice, strain into a chilled martini glass and garnish with a lemon twist.

Six of the best ∞ LONDON CLASSIC COCKTAIL BARS

← THE DORCHESTER
53 Park Lane, Mayfair, London W1A 2HJ
T: 020 7629 8888

AMERICAN BAR AT THE SAVOY
Strand, London WC2R 0BP
T: 020 7836 4343

BLUE BAR AT THE BERKELEY
Berkeley Hotel, Wilton Place, Knightsbridge
London SW1X 7RL, T:020 7235 6000

CLARIDGE'S BAR
Claridge's Hotel, 55 Brook Street, Mayfair
London W1A 2JO, T: 020 7629 8860

DUKE'S HOTEL
35 St. James Place, St. James
London SW1A INY, T: 020 7491 4840

LIBRARY BAR
The Lanesborough Hotel, Hyde Park Corner
London SW1X 7TA, T: 020 7207 5599

TRADITIONAL BEEFEATER DRINKS

Gin and Tonic is a perfect match, the clean taste of the gin enhancing the aromatic bitterness of the tonic water in a quintessentially English drink.

Traditionally the most common mixers for gin were orange squash, ginger beer, peppermint and lime cordials and, of course, tonic water. Of them all, tonic water still reigns supreme in long drinks. No wonder. Gin and Tonic is a perfect match, the clean taste of the gin enhancing the aromatic bitterness of the tonic water in a quintessentially English drink. And, like many other English customs, the Gin and Tonic owes its existence to the British presence in India. During the years of the Raj, British colonials took daily doses of quinine to prevent malaria. They made the bitter flavour of the quinine palatable by adding sugar, soda water and lemon juice. The introduction of gin transformed the medicine into a welcome sundowner and an institution was born.

Returning expats made this exotic drink popular at home and soon all the ingredients were easily available. Commercial production of quinine based tonic water began in the mid-19th century with Erasmus Bond in 1858, followed by Schweppes' Indian Tonic Water in the 1870s. However, modern tonic water contains minute quantities of quinine and one would have to drink 40 Gin and Tonics a day to gain any medicinal benefit.

Gin and Tonic is as popular today as it was in the Gin Palaces of Victorian London. And, whilst there's no longer much call for a gin and peppermint, the gin drinks available at London's traditional bars still reflect long established English tastes and drinking culture.

ROSE'S LIME JUICE

Lauchlin Rose patented a process to preserve lime juice so that it could be taken on long sea voyages to prevent scurvy. A new law which required all ships to carry lime juice as a daily ration for their crews led to the remarkable success of Rose's Lime Juice. It also resulted in British sailors being called 'limeys'. The Gimlet is named after a naval surgeon, Dr. Gimlette, who spiced up his daily ration of lime juice with a measure or two of gin.

THE PERFECT GIN AND TONIC

Beefeater Gin
wedge of lemon or lime
tonic

Completely fill a tall glass with ice
cubes. Add a generous measure of
Beefeater Gin and pour in enough tonic
to fill the glass. Add a freshly cut wedge
of lemon or lime. Stir to release the
juniper flavour and drink immediately.

THE GIMLET

2 shots Beefeater Gin
1 shot Rose's Lime Juice

Pour ingredients into a mixing glass
three quarters filled with ice cubes.
Stir until ice cold. Strain into a chilled
martini glass. Garnish with a slice of
lime peel.

JOHN COLLINS

2 shots Beefeater Gin
1 lemon
crushed ice
1 teaspoon caster sugar
soda water

Squeeze the juice of a lemon into a tall
Collins glass. Add the sugar, the gin and
plenty of ice and stir. Top with soda
water and garnish with 2 lemon slices.

Six of the best ⮎ LONDON GIN PALACES

← THE ARGYLL ARMS
18 Argyll Street, London W1F 7TP
T: 020 7734 6117

THE SALISBURY
90 St. Martin's Lane, London WC2N 4AP
T: 020 7836 5863

PRINCESS LOUISE
208-209 High Holborn, London WC1V 7BW
T: 020 7405 8816

THE RED LION
48 Parliament Street, London SW1 2NH
T: 020 7499 1307

PRINCE ALFRED
5a Formosa Street, London W9 1EE
T: 020 7286 3287

KING'S HEAD
84 Upper Tooting Road, London SW17 7PB
T: 020 8767 6708

BEEFEATER IN LONDON TODAY

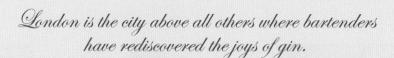

*London is the city above all others where bartenders
have rediscovered the joys of gin.*

Throughout their long history cocktails have gone in and out of fashion. Now cocktails are back and gin is leading the renaissance. London is the city above all others where bartenders have discovered the joys of gin. Indeed it's a city where more and more bars focus totally on gin. Subtle and interesting botanical elements inspire new cocktails that showcase gin's unique personality. A new generation of London bartenders experiment endlessly with new combinations involving fresh fruits of all kinds, unusual spices and herbs. At the same time there's an interest in reinventing the classic gin cocktails and revisiting old favourites with modern eyes. Whether it's a new invention, a trip down memory lane, or playing around with a classic formula, London drinking is always an experience. And Beefeater Gin inspires London's cocktail maestros to new heights.

GIN IN THE KITCHEN

Gin is often used in the kitchen for example by freezing gin and tonic or any other favourite cocktail to make a delicious sorbet. Or showcase gin's flavour profile in a simple seasoning for fish, meat and chicken that is easily made by putting a handful of juniper berries, salt, coriander seeds and citrus peel in a blender and grinding into a coarse powder.

BRAMBLE

(Invented by Dick Bradsell)

2 shots Beefeater Gin
1 shot fresh squeezed lemon juice
1 shot sugar syrup
1 shot Crème de Mure

Shake first 3 ingredients with ice and strain into a crushed ice filled old fashioned glass. Slowly drizzle Crème de Mure through the crushed ice to create a 'marbled effect' and garnish with blackberries and a lemon slice.

THE RASPBERRY COLLINS

Drink created in the 1990's as a seasonal twist on the Tom Collins.

2 shots Beefeater Gin
1 shot lemon juice
$^1/_2$ shot sugar syrup
5 raspberries
soda

Shake all ingredients except soda. Strain into an ice filled tall glass. Top up with soda water. Garnish with a lemon slice and 2 fresh raspberries.

WATERLOO SUNSET

A reworking of the classic champagne cocktail by Dan Warner.

$^3/_4$ shot Beefeater Gin
$^1/_2$ shot elderflower cordial
4 shots Perrier Jouët Champagne
$^1/_4$ shot Crème de Framboise

Stir Beefeater and elderflower cordial in a jug with ice and strain into a flute. Layer the Champagne on top and add Crème de Framboise with a bar spoon and garnish with a speared raspberry.

Six of the best ∞ LONDON STYLE BARS

← LONSDALE
48 Lonsdale Road, London W11 2DE
T: 020 7727 4080

HAWKSMOOR
157 Commercial Street , Whitechapel
London E1 6BJ, T: 020 7247-7392

THE PLAYER
8 Broadwick Street, Soho, London W1F 8HN
T: 020 7494 9125

RONNIE SCOTT'S JAZZ CLUB
47 Frith Street, Soho, London W1D 4HT
T: 020 7439 0747

MONTGOMERY PLACE
31 Kensington Park Road, London W11 2EU
T: 020 7792 3921

MILK & HONEY
61 Poland Street, London W1F 7NU
Reservations required, T: 07000 655 469
(Members only after 11pm)

Published by: Contagious Publishing Limited, The Bond Building, 33 Breadalbane Street, Edinburgh EH6 5JW
on behalf of Allied Domecq Spirits & Wine Limited.

The Beefeater Distillery, 20 Montford Place, Kennington, London SE11 5DE

ISBN 978-0-9557431-0-8

Acknowledgements: Helen Arthur, Nick Blacknell, Angus Bremner, Beth Coates, Clementine Hope, Brian Martin, Iain McIntosh, Desmond Payne, Joanne Smith, Dan Warner, Jackie Law. Picture credits: Guildhall Library, City of London; Museum of London; The Bridgeman Art Library; Mary Evans Picture Library. Design: Contagious. Words: Geraldine Coates.

Be sure

your sins will find you out

James Burrough, 1863